AMAZING LIZARDS

Jayne Pettit

D0723951

SCHOLASTIC INC.
New York Toronto London Auckland Sydney

Photo Credits

ISBN 0-590-43682-1

12 11 10 9 8 7 6 5 4 3   1 2 3 4 5/9

Printed in the U.S.A.   40

First Scholastic printing, December 1990

Contents

Acknowledgments

I would like to express my deepest appreciation to Ann Reit and Amy Scheinberg, my editors at Scholastic, Inc., for their encouragement and sound advice during the development of *Amazing Lizards*.

My special thanks to the following people, whose expertise in the field of herpetology contributed significantly to this project:

John Cadle, Ph.D., Zoology, and Assistant Curator of Herpetology, Academy of Natural Sciences, Philadelphia, PA; Elizabeth Dorey, Administrative Assistant, Reptile Breeding Foundation, Picton, Ontario, Canada; John Groves, Curator of Amphibians, Reptiles, and Birds, Philadelphia Zoological Garden, Philadelphia, PA; Thomas Huff, Executive Director, Reptile Breeding Foundation, Picton, Ontario, Canada; William Lasley, D.V.M., Department of Reproduction, School of Veterinary Medicine, University of California, Davis; Barbara Mathe, Department of Library Services, American Museum of Natural History, New York, NY; Dr. David E. Wildt, Reproductive Physiologist, Department of Animal Health, The National Zoological Park, Washington, D.C.

Finally, I would like to thank Barrie Van Dyck and Bin Pettit, whose wise support gave me the incentive to complete this book.

Geological Timeline

Our planet is very old! Geologists, scientists who study the earth's crust and rock layers, have named the main eras of the earth's history in order to trace the evolution of life on our planet. This timeline will help you to understand.

4,500 million years ago	**Early Precambrian, or Azoic** The era "without life." The earliest era, when no life existed and the earth was just forming.
2,500 million years ago	**Late Precambrian, or Proterozoic** The era of "first life." Life was beginning in the sea. Algae, bacteria, and, later, corals, jellyfish, and sponges came to life.
600 million years ago	**Paleozoic** The "ancient life" era. Many kinds of plants and animals evolved in the sea and, later, on land. Earliest fish, amphibians, reptiles, cone forests, and swamps.
250 million years ago	**Mesozoic** The "middle life" era, or the Age of Reptiles. Dinosaurs, birds, lizards, and flowering plants. Dinosaurs died out at the end of this period.
66 million years ago	**Cenozoic** The "new life" era. Appearance of the first small mammals. Later, grasses, grains, apes, giant land mammals, primitive man, ice ages, and early agriculture.

1
Lizards:
Living Reminders of an Ancient Past

In the warm stillness of a Mediterranean night, a gecko barks, then scurries along a garden wall. High in the trees of a tropical rain forest on the island of Papua, a Flying dragon glides from branch to branch. And across the hot sands of a Southwestern desert, a Sandfish skink "swims" toward its next meal. These reminders of an ancient past — before the age of man — belong to the world of the lizards.

Over three thousand species of lizards exist today in habitats as far north as the arctic regions of Norway, and as far south as the southern tip of Argentina. They are as varied in shape, size, and ornamentation as the areas in which they dwell. Creeping about with the slowness of an alligator, or racing along at a speed of twenty miles an hour, lizards do indeed remind us of a prehistoric time when strange creatures roamed the waters and skies of an infant earth.

Imagine the world as it must have looked 300 million years ago! A world of seas, swamps, and towering forests bursting forth from changing landmasses that twisted and quaked with each new upheaval in the earth's core. In the great oceans, primitive fishes roamed. No living beings inhabited the land, for the creatures of the seas had no need to venture from them.

As the years passed further changes occurred. The climate warmed and the earth's atmosphere became drier. The seas, swamps, and mud pools shrank, forcing some creatures to push onto the land. Gradually these early beings developed lung-like structures that evolved into lungs. Moving easily now between the water and the land, the creatures became the earth's first *amphibians* — water animals that can breathe comfortably on land. Adapting to their new surroundings, they eventually acquired skeletons more suitable for traveling about in search of the abundant plant life that existed.

Fossil remains show us that the earliest amphibians had broad skulls that were flat and heavily armored, and looked much like modern-day crocodiles. They were not graceful creatures, and fossil tracks show that they dragged themselves about. This was no doubt because their appendages, or limbs, had not fully adapted to movement on land.

As the earliest swamps and forests disappeared — about 250 million years ago — the Age of Amphibians came to an end. (Frogs, toads, salamanders, sirens, caecilians, and newts are our only true amphibians today.) The descendants of those primitive beings learned to live, breed, and feed outside of the water. These animals were the first *reptiles*.

Reptiles and their ancestors, the amphibians, differ in many ways. The skin of an amphibian is usually smooth and can absorb as well as release water, while that of a reptile is rough and scaly and can repel water. An amphibian lays its jelly-like eggs in water or damp places, while a reptile's eggs are covered with a hard or leathery shell that allows the young to develop within them on land. These differences enable reptiles to exist independently of the water, while amphibians rely on water for feeding and breeding, emerging only for brief periods of time. Reptiles have undergone great changes during the course of the earth's history — many more than amphibians.

Scientists call the earliest reptiles *cotylosaurs*, or "beginning lizards." These large animals had skeletons much like the earlier amphibians, but in time their bodies underwent many changes to adapt to life on land. Body organs such as the heart and lungs became more complex, and the smooth skin of the amphibian was replaced by a thick, scaly covering. Skulls hardened and lengthened, and the soft eggs laid in water by amphibian ancestors developed hard or leathery shells that could be hatched on land. And, as the cotylosaurs discovered new sources of food, they acquired powerful jaws with which to chew the plant life of their surroundings.

This era, between 66 and 250 million years ago, is known to us as the Age of Reptiles. As our earth was undergoing great changes in climate and environment, it was this group of primitive creatures that became the most powerful life-forms. This is also called the *Mesozoic*, or "middle life," era.

The cotylosaurs of the Age of Reptiles can claim many descendants, each of which had to adapt to the changes taking place around them. One group of animals developed into the remarkably armored reptiles we call turtles and tortoises, both of which still look much like they did millions of years ago. Two other groups of descendants returned to the water. These were the paddle-limbed plesiosaurs and the fish-like ichthyosaurs (or fish lizards). Although both of these are now extinct, their fossil remains show us what they looked like.

Still other lines of descent from the cotylosaurs were the thecodonts. These were small, lizard-like creatures that ran about on their hind legs. Many types of reptiles emerged from the thecodonts. Among these were the crocodilians, the flying reptiles, and the dinosaurs, or "terrible lizards." (Early scientists thought all dinosaurs were types of lizards because of their resemblance to one another. Actually, their skeletons were quite different.) And certainly the most beautiful of all creatures to have descended from those ancient thecodonts are the birds that grace our skies today.

Lizards are the most familiar of all the earth's reptiles. There are as many as 3,751 different species, and they inhabit every continent but Antarctica.

Lizards vary greatly in size. They may be as small as the tiniest gecko, little more than an inch long. Or they may be as large as the Komodo dragon, reaching up to ten feet in length.

Many of these fascinating animals still look as though they belong to an ancient world. Some have prehistoric-looking horns about their heads, snouts, necks, and tails. Others have hides covered with thick, overlapping plates, and huge collars about their necks. Marine iguanas and other large lizards have clawed feet shaped like those of the animals that roamed the earth millions of years ago.

Almost all lizards are noticeably different from their relatives, the snakes. Most obviously, the majority of lizards have limbs, while most snakes do not. Those lizards without limbs do indeed look like snakes. However, they can move their lower eyelids while snakes cannot. Most lizards also possess external ear openings and a tail as long or longer than their bodies.

Both lizards and snakes have scaly skins, backbones called *vertebrae*, and muscles. Both groups of animals have a heart, intestines, liver, and lungs. Certain lizards and snakes are *viviparous*, which means they give birth to live young. But most species are egg-laying. Lizards such as the gecko shed their skins just as snakes do.

Many years ago, an English naturalist named Charles Darwin traveled to the Galápagos Islands, off the western coast of Ecuador in South America. While there, Darwin made extensive notes and drawings of a lizard called the Marine iguana. Darwin was fascinated by its prehistoric appearance and behavior, calling it "a hideous-looking creature of a dirty black color, stupid and sluggish in its movements."

Moving from island to island to observe the unusual lizard, Darwin commented on the iguana's amazing ability to adapt to its surroundings as it crawled over masses of lava rock and dove into the sea. This remarkable behavior added to Darwin's theory of *natural selection*. This theory states that only the strongest and fittest living beings can survive their surroundings.

Several years later, Darwin wrote a book entitled *The Origin of Species*. The book traces the history of the living things of the world and describes the way in which plants, animals, and people must adapt to their environments in order to survive. Today, scientists and environmentalists call Darwin's theory "the survival of the fittest."

Darwin's observations of the Marine iguanas and other animals on the Galápagos Islands convinced him that his theory of natural selection was correct. As he watched those ancient-looking creatures move about in a hot, barren region where food and water were extremely scarce, he concluded that this was the way prehistoric life-forms had battled their environments for millions of years. Darwin's studies also reasoned that those living things that weren't strong enough to cope with their surroundings died, eventually becoming extinct.

Hundreds of millions of years have passed since the first primitive creatures of the sea began evolving into the life-forms that exist in our world today. Throughout those years, countless changes have taken place.

Today's lizards are living reminders of those ancient times when animals — not man — ruled the earth. Scientists are eager to gather new information about these remarkable creatures. They know that there is still much to learn about the development of all living things. As research continues, an increasing number of scientists believe that the lizards can provide important clues to many mysteries surrounding the evolution of life on our planet.

2
Those Amazing Lizards:
Taking a Closer Look

Lizards are amazing creatures. With sixteen families existing in the world today, they differ remarkably in size, shape, color, ornamentation, and behavior. Lizards are capable of living in a variety of habitats. Many are tree dwellers, some bask on rocks near the sea, and still others inhabit the hot, dry regions of the desert. Some lizards can travel as fast as twenty miles an hour, while others barely move at all.

A lizard's body is fascinating. It is covered with scaly skin, its scales being as small and smooth as a gecko's, or as large and plate-like as a monitor's. Scientists believe that this scaly skin helps the lizard to retain water, allowing the animal to control its body temperature. Since the lizard is a cold-blooded creature, its body doesn't adjust to heat and cold as a human body does. Therefore, a lizard practices a behavior called *thermoregulation*, which enables it to adjust its body temperature while it copes with extremes of daytime heat and nighttime cold. When a lizard suns itself, we tend to think it is just lazily relaxing. Actually, it is soaking up warmth to store away for future hours of cold.

Like most reptiles, the lizard sheds its skin several times a year. This shedding occurs in different ways, depending on the species. Small pieces of skin may flake off, or large sections may drop away. A gecko lizard sheds its skin by rubbing it loose, either whole or in pieces, and then eating it.

The lizard's head is quite flexible, as its unusual set of jawbones are connected by a series of elastic muscles. Because of this, the animal can flatten its head easily when squeezing in and out of tight places. An important part of the lizard's head is its tongue, which is used to "sense out" the world about it. This "sensing" allows the creature to detect an enemy, attract a potential mate, or move toward a food source. Openings in the skull enable the lizard to hear, and it appears to have a strong sense of taste and smell.

The lizard's eyes are as keen as the cat's, enabling it to adjust quickly to darkness as well as to light. Most lizards have eyes that are protected by a movable eyelid, although the little gecko lizard has none.

A number of lizards, such as the chameleons, have *zygodactal* feet, with toes pointing both forward and backward. This strange characteristic allows the creatures to climb with great speed and skill. Geckos have tiny, hook-like hairs on the bottoms of their toes that enable them to cling upside down on surfaces as smooth as glass. Most lizards, such as the Fringe-toe, have feet that are well adapted to scurrying across sand. Still others have long, clawed toes that help them to capture prey and to move about on rough terrain.

A great number of lizards can do remarkable things with their tails. Many have *prehensile* tails, or strong, flexible tails that they wrap around tree branches for balance while eating or resting. Others use their tails for balance when running, or to signal a potential mate. Many lizards have the amazing ability to break off their tails in an action called *autotomy*. When this happens, a new tail develops as the old one heals. Scientists have photographed several creatures that had acquired two or even three tails!

Lizards feed on insects and small rodents — although some prefer vegetation and larger animals. An Indonesian monitor lizard called the Komodo dragon can kill prey as large as a small deer or a pig. The Marine iguanas of the Galápagos Islands feed exclusively on food from the sea. Much of their day is spent diving for seaweed and *algae*, which are tiny green plants that live on the surface of the water.

Most lizards are great runners, scurrying about the woods, deserts, grasses, and beaches of the world. As they scamper along they often perform wonderful acrobatic tricks, darting up and down trees and walls and hanging upside down on ceilings.

Lizards can defend themselves in a number of ways. One of the most amazing is the ability of most lizards, such as chameleons, to change color in order to protect themselves. The lizard not only can change color, but can actually take on the exact patterns of the surface it is lying on, whether it be the bark of a tree, the veins of a leaf, or the texture of rocks or sand.

In another defense tactic, most lizards can use their ability to break off their tails. The many nerve endings of the detached tail cause it to jerk and hop about, scaring an enemy into running for its life. Or, the wriggling tail provides a distraction while the lizard darts off.

Most lizards under attack will try to escape by running away. However, if they sense that they are cornered, they will resort to any number of strategies, such as exposing powerful jaws, lashing out with their tails, hissing, or burrowing quickly into the sand or the ground.

When lizards court one another, the male establishes a particular territory and throws out signals to a female as he approaches her. The male Green anole lizard bobs its head up and down and balloons its dewlap, which are folds of skin located at the throat. Geckos use their voices to chirp or bark messages to each other. Other signals might be rapid side-to-side movements of the head or tail. Some males bite, scratch, or flick their tongues toward females to "sense out" information about them.

If a female isn't interested in mating, it may hiss, arch its back, or just move quietly away. When the lizards do mate, some time later (varying from several weeks to a few months), most female lizards will lay a clutch of from one to forty-five eggs, burying them under a rock or a log. Occasionally the eggs are hidden underground. A few females are viviparous and give birth to live young. For example, some Pygmy chameleons and certain Horned lizards bear living offspring. Lizard females give little or no attention to their eggs or to their young.

In several lizard species, females can lay eggs that do not need to be fertilized. This behavior is known as *parthenogenesis* and it is also com-

mon in flies, earthworms, and some fish and amphibians.

Most lizards do not communicate with a voice
other than the hissing sound. The exception is the
remarkable little gecko, which can chirp, click, or
even bark as loudly as a dog.

As we learn more about these unusual creatures,
we increase our appreciation of them. We no
longer think of lizards as an eighteenth-century
scientist once described them: "these foul and
loathsome animals."

The Sixteen Lizard Families

Chisel-teeth lizards or Agamids (approximately 300
  species)
Chameleons (approximately 85 species)
Iguanas (approximately 650 species)
Geckos (approximately 800 species)
Monitors (approximately 31 species)
Snake lizards (31 species)
Whiptail lizards (approximately 225 species)
Wall and Sand lizards (approximately 200 species)
Night lizards (16 species)
Skinks (approximately 1,275 species)
Girdle-tailed lizards (approximately 50 species)
Blind lizards (approximately 4 species)
Xenosaurs (4 species)
Anguids (approximately 75 species)
Beaded lizards (2 species)
Bornean earless lizard (1 species)

3
Agamids and Chameleons: The Camouflage Artists

Scurrying about on the ground, in trees, and even in the waters of tropical rain forests in Africa, Australia, and other warm regions throughout the Old World, 300 species of lizards called agamids can be found. Agamids, like chameleons, can change colors, and some — such as the Flying dragons of India and the South Pacific — swiftly glide from tree to tree with surprising grace. Spiny-tailed agamids who live in the desert areas of Africa and India are also remarkable for their ability to obtain and store water from the sparse plant life around them. The Australian moloch can do the most amazing thing of all the agamids. Within seconds, it can soak up water directly through canals between the scales covering its body!

Agamids look so much like the iguana lizards of our Western Hemisphere that it is difficult to tell them apart. Only scientists can distinguish agamids from iguanas by studying the structure of their teeth. Agamids are often known as Chisel-teeth lizards.

Many agamid lizards display beautiful colors and patterns. Vivid yellows, blues, greens, and oranges blend with tans, browns, and blacks to give the animals striking appearances. Wonderful ornaments decorate most agamids, such as neck frills and dewlaps. Horns, helmets, crests, and large spines adorn the agamids' heads, necks, backs, and tails.

Agamids vary greatly in size. Certain Toad-headed lizards are only about two inches long. The largest of all is the four-and-a-half-foot-long Soa-Soa, which inhabits certain islands in the South Pacific.

Agamid lizards have strong bodies as well as long legs and tails. Their heads are quite large and their tails, which cannot be broken off in self-defense, are usually covered with large scales or spines. These animals have excellent eyesight — stronger than their sense of smell. Desert agamids often carry scales on their eyelids (like eyelashes!) to keep sand from blowing into their eyes.

Agamids are active during the daytime. In deserts and tropical rain forests from Africa to Australia, these animals sun themselves on rocks and tree branches to adjust their body temperatures between daytime and nighttime hours. At night and during the hottest periods of the day, they find shelter under rocks or in crevices or caves.

Agamid lizards live in communities with one male as the leader. The males guard their territories, often changing from their usual brown, gray, or black coloring to a combination of brighter colors — such as blue and orange. A guarding male does this to ward off enemies. Male agamids within a community fight each other over territory, bobbing their heads angrily and whipping their powerful tails. During the mating season females group together. Males then court the leader of a particular group. This mating period occurs only during the rainy months. Female agamids lay between four to six eggs in a single clutch.

The Spiny-tailed lizards of northern Africa and India are large agamids with small heads and flattened bodies. They display many different patterns that may be orange, yellow, green, or red. Spinytails are peaceful animals who inhabit desert regions. Their diet consists mainly of plant life. The young eat insects. From April to June, during the rainy season, females will lay up to fourteen eggs. After hatching, the young stay with their parents for a while.

Among the most unusual of the agamids are the

Frilled lizards of Australia and Papua, and the Flying dragons of the South Pacific. Frilled lizards have a huge "collar" about their necks, which they can stretch straight out to ward off enemies, or to court members of the opposite sex. These animals can also stand on their hind legs and dart off at great speed. The Flying dragons can spread out their sides and use them as wings to fly or glide from tree to tree.

Chameleons are descendants of ancient agamids. However, they differ from today's agamids in several ways. Agamids have very large heads, long necks, and heavy spines on their backs and tails. Chameleons are smaller creatures with flattened bodies and heads. They appear to have no necks and their limbs are long and quite thin. The agamid's eyes and lids are well developed, while those of the chameleon look like little towers and can move independently to focus on prey.

Besides their ability to change into many different colors — more remarkably than the rest of the lizards — chameleons can do other amazing things. They can move their eyes in opposite directions at the same time, and their tongues can stretch out further than the length of their bodies!

Chameleons have peculiar toes, too. On each foot the five toes are arranged in two separate groups — two toes and three toes — for good gripping on tree branches. Their prehensile tails are used to wrap around the branches for balance.

Chameleons like to feed on grasshoppers, spiders, and scorpions. Some larger species eat small birds and mammals.

There is no particular mating season for the chameleon. Females may lay between four and forty eggs. The Dwarf — or Pygmy — chameleons of the mountainous regions of South Africa give birth to live young. Most chameleons like to keep to themselves, although they have a well-developed social system with a male leader who keeps watch over other chameleons who inhabit its territory.

One of the more unusual-looking chameleons is the West African Mountain chameleon, which is blue, green, and tan, with an enormous horned snout and huge eyes. Dwarf chameleons have crests along their sides and along their tails. The Dwarfs shed their skins every three to four weeks. Chameleons living in Madagascar — off the coast of Africa — have many horns on their snouts, which the males use to do battle over females and territory.

Chameleons are popular terrarium pets because of their striking appearance and their amazing habits. They are difficult to keep, however, because they require a special diet of insects, spiders, and scorpions, and must have plant life on which they can practice their climbing techniques. (It's hard to fit tree branches into terrariums!) A chameleon's terrarium must have adequate exposure to sunlight so that the animal can regulate its body heat. All of these factors make a chameleon's survival in captivity a risky business.

4
The Iguanas: Creatures from an Earlier Time

Along the rugged beaches of the Galápagos Islands west of Ecuador, South America, strange-looking animals called Marine iguanas bask lazily in the sun. Moving slowly from rock to rock, these creatures, which filled Charles Darwin's notebooks and sketch pads, soak up the sun's warmth before plunging back into the sea for food. In this dry, tropical region of the world, the land and its inhabitants remind us of the way the earth looked millions of years ago.

Marine iguanas are members of the large iguana family of lizards (650 species in all) that dwell in a wide range of habitats in the Western Hemisphere, including deserts, rain forests, mountains, and seacoasts. The iguanas differ greatly in size.

Some measure a scant two-and-a-half inches in length while others, such as the Marine iguanas, reach almost three feet.

Each iguana species is unique in appearance. One group might be armed with helmets about the head, while another is adorned with horns and crests. Still another sports a scaly collar around the neck, spines along the back and tail, or dewlaps at the throat, which inflate and turn a brilliant hue when the animal becomes excited. Some iguanas are striking in color. The Anole lizard boasts bright yellows and oranges blended with tan markings, while the patterned body of the Collared lizard is rich with tones of turquoise and blue.

Many of these animals can do remarkable things. For example, Basilisk iguanas love to charge across the surface of lakes and ponds. Folds along their toes extend like webs, allowing them to skim along on hind legs that propel them forward. They are amusing to watch as they appear to *run* on top of the water. Marine iguanas swim long distances out to sea or from island to island, peacefully submerging themselves for long periods of time. Desert iguanas dart across the sands at speeds of up to fifteen miles an hour, running on strong hind legs to avoid capture by an enemy.

Most species of iguanas live in communities. Males protect their territories carefully by doing ritual battle with other males — standing on hind legs, bobbing their heads, hissing and snapping their tails as they erect their crests or inflate their dewlaps. Most of these battles are ceremonial. Iguanas seldom hurt one another.

A large number of iguana species belong to the Spiny lizard group. Most of these are in Mexico, and a few can be found scurrying about in the American Southwest. Spiny lizards occupy the widest range of iguana habitats. They are quite at home in desert regions, grasslands, and brush, as well as wooded areas and mountains. Spiny lizards such as the Eastern and Western Fence lizards sun themselves for long periods on fence posts, rocks, and tree trunks. Feeding on insects, spiders, and tasty leaves or buds, these animals actually measure five inches or less, although their rough scales make them look bigger than they are. Many of the creatures have rough scales on their backs, and the males' throats are a beautiful blue. Spiny lizards of the desert feed on cactuses, eating the whole plant — spines and all!

Spiny lizards display curious defense tactics. When threatened by enemies, males and females arch the scales on their backs to make themselves look much larger than they are. If this doesn't frighten off the other animals, the lizards will bob their heads up and down with amazing speed to scare them away. When fighting for territory or for attractive females, the males flatten their bodies to extend them, showing the bright blue of their undersides.

Fringe-toed lizards, natives of Arizona, are only active during the cool hours of the morning. Otherwise, they bury themselves in the sand. Swimming through the loose sand, their bodies move along quicky and easily. Flaps at the nose and ears keep sand from entering. These amazing little animals have hearing and a sense of smell sensitive enough to detect prey hidden underground. When threatened, a Fringe-toe flattens its body at an angle to reveal a black spot that, for some mysterious reason, frightens off an attacking enemy.

Tiny earless lizards, such as the Gridiron and the Zebra tail, also thrive in the American Southwest, protecting themselves by waving their banded tails back and forth frantically. They are also fast runners, outracing an enemy at twenty miles an hour!

Seven species of Horned lizards live in the United States. These are unique because they can bear live young — often up to thirty-two at a time. The Texas species can survive in populated areas, although it sometimes confronts the roar of a Saturday morning lawn mower. No problem! It simply flattens itself like a pancake until the crisis passes by.

The foot-long Collared lizards and Leopard lizards of the American Southwest run on their hind legs, and feed on large insects as well as on other smaller lizards. Collared lizards are active only in extreme heat and can stand blazing temperatures that would kill most other lizards. Females change color three to four days after mating. Scarlet spots appear on their bodies until a clutch of up to twenty-four eggs is laid. Males drive other full-grown lizards from their territories, but allow juveniles to stay.

Spiny-tailed lizards are among the smallest of the iguanas, measuring about two-and-a-half inches at birth, and four to eight inches as adults. Sawtooth scales decorate their long tails, which, according to superstition, can saw through a thick tree trunk.

Roaming the hot sands of the Mojave Desert in the American Southwest, as well as Angel Island off the coast of Mexico, there's a fascinating iguana called the Chuckwalla. This amazing animal has unusually flabby skin for a lizard. When threatened by a predator, the Chuckwalla will race into a rock, jam itself into a tight crevice, and suck in air. It blows up like a balloon, making it impossible for an enemy to pull it out!

In many areas of Central and South America today, iguanas are falling victim to the whims of man. For example, in the American Southwest, many species are threatened by the conversion of natural areas into residential and commercial development. Green iguanas from Central American countries suffer mass exportation each year as pets. Few of these survive captivity. Thousands of Green iguanas and other iguana species are being wiped out as the tropical rain forests in which they live are destroyed. Of all the species, the Green iguanas have suffered the most because they are hunted extensively for their delicate meat, which tastes very much like chicken. Latin Americans call these lizards *gallino de palo* or "chicken of the tree." They have relied on this delicacy for thousands of years.

In Central America, efforts are underway to protect the Green iguanas by encouraging local farmers to raise these animals on ranches similar to those for chickens. Scientists are also trying to convince farmers to save the tropical rain forests that are home to the animals.

Organizations such as the Green Iguana Foundation and the Smithsonian Tropical Research Institute have found that iguanas breed quickly in specially designed structures where sunlight and proper food and nesting conditions exist. One researcher, Dr. Dagmar Werner of the Green Iguana Foundation, devised a laying nest in which 95 percent of the eggs hatched after incubation, which dramatically increased the birth rate of these prized creatures.

In recent efforts, the iguanas have been kept on breeding ranches until the age of one year. After

Gila monster

Green iguana emerging from its shell

Russian spider gecko

Immediately after emerging from its shell, the Green iguana hatchling is still covered with specks of dirt.

Collared lizard

Chuckwalla

Madagascar painted gecko

Banded gecko

Yarrow's spiny lizard

Short-horned lizard

Fat-tailed gecko

Young Western skink with blue tail

that, they are set free to roam the forests, and farmers have been advised to limit their hunting until the population has a chance to increase. Scientists hope that by raising iguanas on ranches and working to save the rain forest, the farmers will keep their valuable food source and the treasured iguana population will be allowed to flourish once again.

5
Geckos:
The Champion Acrobats

Geckos are the acrobats of the lizard world. They move with lightning speed, darting in and out of rocky crevices, scaling tree trunks, and scooting across walls with remarkable ease. Geckos can even climb vertical panes of glass and hang upside down on ceilings! Microscopic hair-like bristles on the undersides of their feet give them this great clinging power.

There are eight hundred species of geckos living in the warm regions of the Eastern and Western Hemispheres. The smallest measures just a little over an inch, and the largest is slightly under two feet. Many are quite colorful and have beautiful patterns on their bodies. The Banded geckos of our Southwest and the Reticulated (a kind of netlike pattern) geckos of northern Mexico are striking in appearance, as are Australia's Marbled geckos and the Yellow-heads of southern Florida and the Caribbean.

A gecko's body is flat, and its eyes are very large, with transparent eyelids that look like contact lenses. After a gecko consumes a hearty meal of insects (or, in some cases, small birds or mammals), it carefully cleans its face and eye "lenses" with its tongue. A comical sight! The thousands of tiny, invisible hairs on the gecko's feet enable it to cling to any surface while it rests or basks in the sun. As with snakes, geckos shed their skins periodically.

Unlike other lizards and members of the reptile family, geckos are wonderfully vocal. In fact, their name comes from the wonderful sounds made by an Oriental species that seems to say "geh-co." Some geckos chirp, others croak or quack, and still others bark so loudly they can waken people from a sound sleep in the middle of the night. Geckos can be heard from dusk to early evening when they set up quite a fine chorus that builds to a pitch, and then stops suddenly just before nightfall. It is then that these little animals, which are mostly nocturnal, go about the serious business of hunting for food.

Geckos are secretive in nature and are better at avoiding than at fighting predators. When lightly grasped by a human (which is very hard to do because of their swift movements), or attacked by an enemy, geckos break off sections of their skin in order to escape. Geckos can also break off their tails if necessary to avoid capture. As with many other lizards, they also will change color to blend in with their surroundings and hide from enemies. The flying geckos of Southeast Asia escape from predators by gliding from one tree to another, like the Flying dragons of the South Pacific.

In the mating season, male geckos will do battle with one another, biting and flicking their tails violently until the strongest emerges as the winner. Pairs of geckos will then occupy fixed territories and defend themselves against enemies until the female lays its eggs in cracks or crevices of rocks, usually one or two at a time in a clutch. Between May and August, the female lays eggs four or five times, with a period of two to four weeks between each laying. The most curious fact about the egg-laying process is that some female geckos lay their eggs at a communal site. Nearly one hundred Fan-toed gecko eggs were found in one rocky crevice in Israel!

Geckos are quite at home with people. In fact, these funny little creatures are a welcome sight to home owners because they hunt garden pests. Having no fear of people, they often sneak aboard cargo ships, where they become stowaways and accidental migrants to other areas. But wherever they may chance to land, geckos are quick to adapt to their new surroundings.

Geckos have scattered themselves throughout the world in a wide range of areas. In the Western Hemisphere they can be found in parts of our Southwestern states, further south into Mexico and Central America, and on down into most of South America. In the Eastern Hemisphere, geckos exist throughout Africa, the Middle East, and the subcontinent of India, as well as in Indonesia, Australia, and New Zealand.

Geckos are at home under rocks and stones, in trees, or in holes in the sand or ground, their clawed toes excellently suited for digging and shoveling. These amazingly adaptable animals have colonized a wide variety of habitats, ranging from deserts to steppes (level, treeless plains), from grasslands and rocky crevices to tropical rain forests and even high mountain areas. One type, the Tibetan gecko, can survive in the Himalayas at altitudes usually too cold for a reptile. Geckos continue to migrate around the world, traveling on fishing and cargo boats, as well as ocean liners. The Turkish gecko was carried all the way from its home on the Mediterranean coast and now inhabits South America!

6
Monitors:
Komodo Dragons and Their Cousins

Monitors have been known to man for thousands of years. Ancient Egyptians drew pictures of them on monuments and other works of art. Linnaeus, the great eighteenth-century botanist, made a study of these fierce-looking lizards. The dragons that so often appeared in early maps, myths, and legends were probably monitors.

Monitors live in the warm regions that stretch from Africa to New Guinea, the Philippines, and Australia. One of the most remarkable things about these lizards is that they can adapt to almost any environment as long as it is a warm one. Some monitors live in rain forests, some are desert-dwellers, and still others prefer the plains. All are excellent swimmers, climbers, and runners.

Although there are thirty-one species of monitors, varying greatly in size from as small as four inches to lengths of more than nine feet, they have many common characteristics. The heads of most species are tapered, with long, slender necks. Monitors have strong legs, full bodies, and thick, powerful tails, which they use for balance. Their tails are also used in battles with predators, as well as in the water where they become rudders while the animals swim. Monitors use their teeth and long, sharp claws as weapons. Most monitors have yellow spots, bands, and patterns. Some display other colors. For instance, the Nile monitor of Egypt is a beautiful blue or green. Monitors are mostly daytime animals that feed on other animals, swallowing them whole just as snakes do. Crocodile and turtle eggs are also a favorite food.

Female monitors lay up to fifty-seven eggs in a clutch, burying them in the ground or in the hollows of trees. These eggs sometimes measure six inches long, as do those of the Komodo dragon. Scientists know very little about the mating behavior of these animals and have little information about their breeding habits.

The Desert monitor, inhabiting dry regions from the African Sahara to Pakistan, lives in holes and defends itself with a remarkably strong tail.

The Nile monitor of Africa is a fine swimmer and diver. It feeds on fish, snails, and mussels and, like many of its relatives, delights in eating crocodile eggs. Both the Desert and the Nile monitors average about six feet in length.

The Bengal monitors of the Indian Subcontinent and Indonesia are great climbers. The males often engage in wrestling matches when fighting over a female.

Certainly the most primitive-looking of any of the monitors is the nine- to ten-foot-long Komodo dragon, which lives only on the island of Komodo and other tiny islands in the South Pacific. It is the largest of the world's lizards and is related to two Australian lizards.

Some of the other monitors that inhabit the South Pacific are the Two-banded, the rare Papua, the Short-tailed, and the Dwarf monitors.

Those monitors known as the Earless monitors are of great interest to scientists today because of their remarkable resemblance to snakes. Zoologists believe the Earless monitors may have descended from the snake lizards of long ago, which had long bodies and hidden eyes. Mystery has surrounded these fascinating beings for years.

The monitors' greatest predators are humans. People who live near the monitors' habitats have relied upon them for their rich meat as well as for their eggs. Fats and oils from the monitors' bodies have been used by the Chinese to produce medicines. Monitor skins have been used to make leather products.

7
Skinks, Whiptails, and Other Curious Creatures

What wonderful variety we find in the world of the lizards. Big lizards, small lizards, worm-like lizards, and dragon-like lizards! And all of them are remarkable in some unique way. Think about the amazing way in which these cold-blooded animals can regulate their body temperatures. Or think about the way agamids, chameleons, and many other species of lizards can change color to camouflage against an enemy. Or how about the way they grow new tails to replace those that have broken off? Another extraordinary tactic!

The remarkable lizards and their unusual ways are just too numerous to be able to discuss within each species. This chapter will highlight a few groups not already mentioned, and will point out something special about each of them.

Whiptail Lizards. The Whiptails are also known as jungle runners and race runners. They are active during the daytime hours, living in tropical rain forests, swamps, deserts, and grasslands, in the Western Hemisphere. Some, such as the Dragon and the Cayman lizards, are fine swimmers and spend much time in the water. These lizards eat small mammals, birds, fish, tadpoles, snails, and some plants. In this species, the males take on brilliant colors during the mating season to show off for the females.

Wall and Sand Lizards. This species is a very active and fast-moving one, but only for a few hours each day. This is because their bodies can function only in extremely high temperatures. Some live in crevices in rocks or cracks in walls and have adapted to these tight spots by evolving flattened bodies. These lizards feed on snails, worms, and snakes, as well as small rodents and plants.

Night Lizards. Night lizards dwell in warm regions of the American Southwest, Mexico, Central America, and the West Indies. Living in rocky crevices and caves, Night lizards like secrecy and tend to hide from humans. They are another of the unusual lizards that give birth to living young. Several species of Night lizards are even more remarkable in that they are made up entirely of females — they lay eggs that need *not* be fertilized by males.

Skinks. Skink lizards are indeed strange and unusual creatures. Of the more than 1,200 species that exist, they have little in common other than the fact that they live only in tropical and temperate climates. Most skinks have smooth, overlapping layers of skin on their heads and bodies, small eyes (which in some species are nonfunctioning), and short tongues that are slightly notched.

These strange-looking animals can be found in both the Eastern and Western Hemispheres. They inhabit deserts as well as forests. Some burrow, others live in trees, and many, like the sandfish, swim along in the sand, looking every bit like a snake. Skinks also love to swim in water. One species, called the Marine skink, dives and can stay submerged for some time to hide from enemies. Some skinks eat insects, while others, like the Australian Blue-tongue (it really is blue!), feed on plants. Green blood skinks actually have green blood.

Girdle-tailed Lizards. The Girdle-tails are un-usual because through the course of evolution, they have acquired three distinctly different body shapes in order to adapt to their particular environment. These animals live only in Africa and on its neighboring island of Madagascar. The first group, the Armadillo lizards, are covered with sharp, pointed spines and have developed a unique way to avoid their enemies: When cornered, they push themselves into the cracks of rocks, inflate their bodies or curl up into a ball, and are almost impossible to get out. The second group, the Cape red-tail, has a very different body, which is quite flat. Those in the third group have long bodies and tails, and are snake-like in appearance, with tiny limbs or none at all. Girdle-tails are egg-layers and plant-eaters. A few of the species will also feed on small animals.

Blind Lizards. The Blind lizards of Mexico have eyes hidden under their skin. Little is known about these creatures, because they are so secretive, but scientists have discovered that these egg-laying inhabitants of tropical rain forests are insectivores.

Xenosaurs. The Xenosaur (pronounced zen-o-soar) lizards of Guatemala, Mexico, and China are quite lazy, slow-moving, and secretive. These curious creatures sneak about in the shade, or at the end of the day before darkness falls. They like to rest in shallow waters or in tree branches that overhang the water. Xenosaurs like to eat small fishes, tadpoles, and flying ants. They are fierce biters, but are not poisonous.

Anguids. Anguid lizards exist throughout a wide area in warm regions of the world. They come in many shapes and sizes, ranging from short and chubby to long and thin. Some anguids have only tiny limbs. Others have none at all, resembling worms and snakes. Many anguids dwell on the ground, or burrow in sand or under rocks. Others can be found in trees. Anguids are mostly egg-layers, but here again they vary in habit. There are some groups that give birth to as many as twenty-six live young at a time! These animals feed on an amazing variety of foods. Anguids will consume small lizards, scorpions, spiders, tadpoles, animal and bird eggs, wasps, grasshoppers, and more. Those species that live further north hibernate during the winter months.

Beaded Lizards. There are only two known types of Beaded lizards. The Mexican variety inhabits the west coast of that country and the America Gila (pronounced heel-a) monster is found in the Southwestern United States and Mexico. Some of these lizards prefer tropical habitats, while others live in desert areas. Both kinds are capable of inflicting painful bites and on rare occasions, humans have died from the wounds. The venom from these animals can cause temporary paralysis to the human heart or respiratory system, as well as severe pain or numbness. Both groups feed on small mammals, reptile and bird eggs, insects, other lizards, and frogs. Beaded lizards usually move about at dusk, enjoying the cooler temperatures. Females lay up to thirteen eggs at a time during summer.

Bornean Earless Lizards. Of the sixteen families of lizards, this is the only family that has but a single species. The Borneans look much like the Beaded lizards but differ in the nostrils; those of the Borneans are placed on the top of the snout. The animals do not have outside ear openings. Scientists have had difficulty studying these strange creatures because they are so secretive and hard to observe.

Tuataras. Enter, the mystery guest! During the past forty years, herpetologists have had great fun arguing about the ancestry of a fascinating creature known as the Tuatara. Once an inhabitant of a great portion of New Zealand, the animal is now near extinction on twenty or so small islets off the New Zealand shores. Native Maoris gave the Tuatara its name, which translates as "peaks on the back." Once thought of as a true lizard, the Tuatara is actually in a different class, and scientists continue to debate over which class it belongs in. This little two-foot reptile looks like a lizard but differs in the structure of its vertebrae and skull. Yet one clue leads us to believe that our mystery guest may be a link to a very ancient past: Its jaw "teeth" are not developed teeth at all, but are merely jagged structures in the animal's jawbone. This kind of formation was typical of reptiles that existed 140 million years ago.

Bedding themselves down in the empty nests of island shore birds, Tuataras sun themselves during the day and scavenge for beetles and other insects during the night. One of the most amazing facts concerning these creatures is that they are capable of living 120 years or more!

8
Lizards and Humans: Secrets for Survival

For millions of years, lizards have been able to survive the various ages of change in the world. But humans have taken a heavy toll on many species of lizards.

Hundreds of thousands of Green iguanas from Central America and chameleons from Africa, Australia, and other warm regions of the Old World are sold into captivity each year as pets and later die from improper food or living conditions. The Green iguana and the monitor have been highly prized for thousands of years as rich sources of meat and eggs. And other lizards are sought to make leather from their skins or for their fats and oils, which can be used in the manufacture of medicines.

Science must find ways to protect these species without endangering the lives and needs of those people in the world who depend upon them for food and medicines.

Researchers have found that it's possible to serve the needs of man as well as those of the lizard species, for instance, by encouraging farmers in Central America to raise iguanas on ranches, rather than hunt them to extinction. Other species of lizards can be saved by enacting laws that will impose quotas on the killing of the animals. Laws such as these would enable certain numbers of lizards to be killed each year for food and medicines without endangering the existence of those needed for breeding and propagation.

Recent discoveries in the medical field reveal that lizards may be of great benefit to human lives. In 1985, Dr. Georg (pronounced Gay-org) Stacher of the University of Vienna in Austria used a substance taken from the skin of an Australian lizard to produce a serum called caerulein. Patients given doses of caerulein were able to resist pain as effectively as they would have if they had been injected with morphine or other pain killers. These studies suggest that in the near future, patients may be relieved of the pain associated with cancer and heart disease.

In other studies, heart surgeons in the United States, Japan, and the Soviet Union are experimenting with a revolutionary kind of laser surgery based on the primitive structure of the heart and circulatory systems of lizards, snakes, and turtles. By creating microscopic holes in the left ventricle of a human heart, surgeons such as Dr. Mahmood Mirhoseini of St. Luke's Hospital in Milwaukee, Wisconsin, create channels through which blood can flow freely into damaged areas of the heart and throughout a patient's circulatory system. This remarkable process has produced excellent results and is a far less complicated and dangerous type of surgery than the coronary bypass technique in practice today. "One of our first patients was done almost two years ago, and his heart is working nicely," reports Dr. Mirhoseini. "In fact, the areas where we lased channels [to open them] are getting more blood than the sections in which we did conventional bypasses." (See "Leapin' Lizards! This Doc Zaps Hearts," by John Langone, in *Discover* magazine, August 1987, pp. 56–61.)

These and other discoveries should convince us that people and lizards, as well as other animals, can be of great benefit to one another. But their survival, and ours, depends upon our efforts to conserve the natural resources of this planet on which we live.

Lizards are indeed amazing creatures. With their endless variations in size, shape, coloration, ornamentation, habit, and habitat, they give us cause for much interest, study, and scientific research. What secrets do these primitive-looking creatures hide? What are their undiscovered links with an ancient past? What will be the next breakthrough in medical science that might prove them to be of further benefit to humankind? And how will we protect them so that they will keep their important place in nature's food chain?

Scientists continue their search for the vital clues that will answer these questions. Many mysteries have yet to be solved concerning the amazing world of the lizards.

Glossary

Adaptation   The ways in which animals adjust to their environments, such as coping with extreme heat or surviving with a limited water or food supply.

Alga(e)   A primitive kind of plant that lies on or near the surface of the water. Algae are a rich food source and may be microscopic or larger in size, such as kelp and other seaweeds.

Amphibian   An animal whose life cycle includes an aquatic stage.

Arboreal   Living in trees.

Autotomy   The ability some lizards have to break off their tails when attacked.

Bask   To lie in one position for a period of time to absorb the heat of the sun.

Carnivore An animal that eats other animals.

Clutch The eggs laid by a single lizard at one time.

Colonize To move to a new area and establish a new population.

Dewlap A fold of skin that hangs from the throat. In a lizard, it can be inflated to send a signal to another lizard or predatory animal.

Display An animal behavior that sends out signals to another animal to communicate in battle or in mating, such as the way lizards bob their heads or wave their tails.

Environment An animal's surroundings, including the climate, food sources, and water supply.

Evolve The way in which living things go through changes during the course of history.

Fertilize To unite a female egg with a male sperm.

Fossil The remains of an animal or plant that is preserved in rock.

Geologist A scientist who studies the earth's crust and rock layers.

Habitat The natural home of an animal or plant.

Herpetology A branch of zoology in which scientists study reptiles and amphibians.

Home Range   The area in which an animal lives.

Insectivore   An animal that eats insects. Many lizards are insectivores.

Juvenile   Sexually immature.

Marine   Living in the sea.

Migration   The movement of animals from one place to another.

Molt   To shed skin before replacing with a new layer.

Natural Selection.   A theory that states that only the strongest and fittest living beings can survive their surroundings.

Naturalist   A person who studies nature.

Nocturnal   Active at night (such as most of the geckos).

Omnivore   An animal that eats animals as well as plants.

Organ   An internal part of an animal that serves a particular function, such as the heart or lungs.

Oviparous   Bearing eggs that hatch outside of the body.

Parthenogenesis   A form of reproduction in which a female egg develops without being fertilized.

Prehensile   Describes the body limb of an animal that can be used for grasping or wrapping around a tree branch, such as the tail of a chameleon.

Rain Forest   A tropical forest that receives a large amount of rainfall within a single year.

Reptile   A cold-blooded vertebrate whose body is covered with scales or plates.

Scale   A thin, flat, plate-like structure. Many scales combined make up the covering for animals such as lizards, snakes, and fish.

Terrarium   An enclosure to keep small animals in a natural setting.

Terrestrial   Living on land.

Territory   An area an animal will protect and defend against other animals.

Thermoregulation   The method cold-blooded animals use to adjust their body temperatures to safe levels in order to survive.

Ventricle   A chamber in the heart that releases the blood supply to the arteries.

Vertebrate   An animal with a spinal column, such as fish, birds, reptiles, amphibians, and mammals.

Viviparous   Giving birth to live young.

Zygodactyl   Having toes on the same foot that face in opposite ways, some pointing forward and some pointing backward.

Bibliography

Books

Bakker, Robert T. *The Dinosaur Heresies*. New York: William Morrow, 1986.

Bellairs, August d'A. *The Life of Reptiles*. 2 vols. London: Weidenfeld and Nicholson, 1969.

Burkhardt, Gordon, and Stanley Rand, eds. *Iguanas of the World*. Park Ridge, NJ: Noyes Publications, 1982.

Carroll, Robert. *Vertebrate Paleontology and Evolution*. San Francisco: W. H. Freedman, 1988.

Cogger, H. G. *Reptiles and Amphibians of Australia*. 3rd ed. Sydney, Australia: A. H. and A. W. Reed, 1983.

Colbert, Edwin H. *The Age of Reptiles*. New York: W. W. Norton, 1965.

Cox, Barry. *Prehistoric Animals*. Toronto: Bantam Books, 1970.

Darwin, Charles. *The Voyage of the Beagle*. New York: B. F. Collier and Son, 1937.

Goin, C. G., O. B. Goin, and G. R. Zugg. *Introduction to Herpetology*. San Francisco: W. H. Freedman, 1984.

Halliday, Tim, and Kraig Adler. *The Encyclopedia of Reptiles and Amphibians*. Oxford, England: Equinox, 1987.

Huey, R. B., E. R. Pianka, and T. W. Schoener, eds. *Lizard Ecology*, Cambridge: Harvard University Press, 1983.

Mattison, Chris. *Lizards of the World*. New York: Facts on File, 1989.

Mertens, Robert. *The World of Amphibians and Reptiles*. New York: McGraw-Hill, 1982.

Patterson, Rod. *Reptiles of Southern Africa*. Capetown, South Africa: C. Struik and Company, 1987.

Schmidt, Karl P., and Robert F. Inger. *Living Reptiles of the World*. Garden City, NY: Doubleday and Company, 1957.

Sharell, Richard. *The Tuatara, Lizards and Frogs of New Zealand*. London: Collins Publishing, 1966.

Spellenberg, Ian F., *Biology of Reptiles*. Glasgow, NY: Chapman and Hall, 1982.

Welch, Kenneth. *Handbook of Maintenance of Reptiles in Captivity*. Malabar, Fla.: R. E. Krieger, 1987.

Welch, Kenneth. *Herpetology of Africa*. Malabar, Fla.: R. E. Krieger, 1985.

Journals, Bulletins, and Periodicals

Benton, Michael M. "The Demise of a Living Fossil?" *Nature*, vol. 323(6091) (October, 1986), p. 762.

Bogert, C. M., and R. M. del Campo. "The Gila Monster and its Allies." *Bulletin of the American Museum of Natural History*, vol. 109(1) (January, 1986), p. 238.

Browne, Malcolm W. "The Fierce and Ugly Komodo Dragon Fights On." *The New York Times* (June 24, 1986), pp. C-1, C-3.

Champion, Dale. "How Taxpayers Help Wildlife." *San Francisco Chronicle* (September 11, 1985), p. C-1.

"Farm-Bred Iguanas Seen as Food Source." *The New York Times*; *The Gazette*, Montreal, Canada (September 8, 1984). (Smithsonian project).

"Feeling No Pain." *Cincinnati Enquirer* (August 31, 1985), p. C-1.

Grusen, Lindsey. "A Plan to Save the Iguanas and the Rain

Forests in the Bargain." *The New York Times* (August 22, 1989), p. C-4.

"Have Your Iguanas and Eat 'Em Too." *Discover* (November, 1986), p. 7.

Kluge, A. L. "Parthenogenesis in Lizards." *Museum of Zoology*, University of Michigan, vol. 152 (1) (January, 1976).

"Lizards Give a Morphine-like Decapeptide." *The Medical Post*, Toronto, Canada (January 8, 1985).

Langone, John. "Leapin' Lizards: This Doc Zaps Hearts." *Discover* (August, 1987), pp. 56–61.

Lasley, William, PhD., University of California (Davis). Letter in response to listed questions posed by the author, February 23, 1989.

Newman, Don. "The Tuatara, 'Old Beak Head,' May Be Neither Old Nor a Beak Head." *Moko*, Wellington, New Zealand (February, 1987), p. 6.

Index

About the Author

Jayne Pettit is an educator and free-lance writer whose articles have been published in *Cobblestone, The Valley Forge Journal,* and *The Quechee Times*. She holds a master's degree in elementary education, and has taught in public and private school classrooms for sixteen years. Ms. Pettit is active in numerous conservation groups. She has three children and lives with her husband in Vermont.